AF230064

SONNETS

Poems on the Death of an Abyssinian Cat

by

Duncan Newcomer

Goose River Press
Waldoboro, Maine

Copyright © 2022 Duncan Newcomer

All rights reserved. No part of this book may be reproduced in any form without written permission from the publisher, except by a reviewer who may quote brief passages in a review to be printed in a newspaper or magazine.

"These poems were originally published under the title 'Haiku for Sonnets' by the online magazine ReadTheSpirit."

Library of Congress Card Number: 2024936658

ISBN: 978-1-59713-275-6

First Printing, 2024

Leslie Moore created the print of Sonnets used for the cover of this book. She is an artist and poet. Her most recent book is *Grackledom*.

Published by
Goose River Press
3400 Friendship Road
Waldoboro ME 04572
e-mail: gooseriverpress@gmail.com
www.gooseriverpress.com

Dedication

This book is dedicated to Eileen Sypher,
dear friend of mine and dear to her four,
count them, in a row, Bichon Frise dogs,
that she and her husband, John Yrchik,
ministered to on their shared earthly journey.
Let us name them in this dedication as well:
Bindu, Zoe, Leela and Maggie.

Foreword

Sonnets, The Death of an Abyssinian Cat

*Spare, raw, exquisite, these elegiac haiku speak for all of us who have lost
our beloved animals.*

—Eileen Sypher

The theme of an elegy. The form of a haiku. But elegies are usually not for
cats, and haiku mostly have a set number of syllables.

Yet the pain of parting with your cat or your dog is both deep and unique. It
is a grief most of us keep to ourselves. It is magnified because we live inside
with them, and with our birds and turtles, sometimes fish and snakes. Up
here in Maine, in the old days, the animal barn and the household were con-
nected against the winter. In even older days, many of the necessary animals
lived right in our dwellings as well, their warmth important for us. From
gerbils to horses, we physically love and spiritually bond with animals that
are not us. We rarely speak of this when they die. We don't know what to
say. They were mainly silent with us and now we are silent without them.

So, raw haiku, renegade haiku, all with the tone of elegy, might be a new
form of language for an ancient grief. Try them yourself.

When my wife and I drove home from the veterinary clinic after Sonnets had
stretched out her front paws and died, I was numb and silent. Some months
later these awkward but apt little phrases came to me. Over some weeks
there were more and more. It was like playing with Sonnets again. I decided
to call them Raw Haiku.

"Duncan," writes the English professor, Dr. Sypher and the ordained minis-
ter, Rev. Eileen, "is a poet, preacher, psychotherapist, who probes with rare
words of love, what few of us are able to: the raw edges of this awful grief.
He makes Sonnets famous 'for sad people everywhere.' These poems open
worlds."

1

Are you ready? Ready
to go up the stairs, eat a treat,
make my life?

2

Right now, under the bedside lamp,
still room made
on bed for you.

3

Can you still jump
there?
Back and forth you tremble.

4

Yes, I would at times
hold your paw as we slept.
Not a third thing, just us.

5

There with your E.T. ears,
I would always come back to you,
there with your E.T. ears.

6

If I had fur like you
but inside,
lick my heart?

7

They say it is best
to put the cat down.
This far? I say.

8

Twelve years never gone.
Two days gone now.
This just doesn't add up.

9

When they see your cat face
they stop doing what they were.
They don't know why.

10

It's your war dance,
chasing this feather on a string.
We take off kite-like.

11

You, Abyssinian cat, round half circle
                                          on bed,
me, tall standing man, white hair,
breeze breaks curtains, your left paw
                                                   stretching.

12

**Of course I talked to you,
but like Tao,
silence was knowing.**

13

**Leave box of tissues
anywhere now.
No table-jumping.**

14

**Gripping grief
even little paws
scimitar claws.**

15

**Last prayer
at end of day,
you raised my spirit.**

16

**Skunk smell outside,
acrid air everywhere,
I keep breathing grief.**

17

I've never caught a fish
with my hands,
nor this grief.

18

As if roaring you yawn,
a tiger awakes, teeth and claws,
then back to sleep.

19

**Moving square of sun
on floor, then higher
on chair, closer for you.**

20

Framed glass door
your place of view
empty now, seeing nothing.

21

My head bowed on yours
our two griefs one
lost each other, but you lost you.

22

**Shall I bring you
my emptiness now
or later?**

23

**These minutes of joy
did they run out
like the ticking clock?**

24

In dozens of Chinese verbs
overtones of grieving,
like Shakespeare, Sonnets.

25

I've had a few
of your white whiskers
retrieved on my wood lamp base.

26

**Of course the sunlight
shown through your ears.
We could all hear it.**

27

**The dark side of moon
still full
wanes when?**

28

**In bed middle
no cat circle
nothing to curve around.**

29

Stepping slowly
to heaven
did we leave anything behind?

30

I look over assured
your absence
present.

31

Head to head
I breathe full of mourn
no air left inside.

32

So, a sonnet for Sonnets.
You, twelve years long.
Where is the couplet?

33

So, it is the next room
where I will see you again,
the next room.

34

I experience you in these words
like the room
you just left.

35

**Exist in these words
Cat Tao Cat Tao Cat Tao?
Lick my hand.**

36

I had all the language.
You had not a word.
You are how we are together now.

37

Tea and cookies
Tea and cookies
Why distract myself?

38

**High bed near window
open air
this night falls.**

39

**It was the
cool drop on your nose,
reassuring.**

40

**Everything was OK.
I had my cat
at least.**

41

**Such joy
my brain a sieve
my face wet.**

42

**Your nostrils like
pin holes, but they put
the last needle in your leg.**

43

No, I won't grieve
forever.
I won't live that long.

44

**Water-bones
do not exist
anywhere but in me.**

45

There's a place for us.
It isn't here
yet.

46

**So, Sonnets, once on an Indian
Reservation an old man
told me he only called his dog "dog."**

47

Let's get this straight then.
Are we talking about you or me?
What? Not talking, tail not straight.

48

There is a softness in this morning air.
Dew sparkles still on ground.
You, nowhere, neither lost nor found.

49

**That morning parallelogram
of sunlight you occupied
all morning misses you.**

50

**You sure did sleep a lot
sleep a lot
sleep a lot.**

51

**Your short golden hairs all
over old green wool blanket.
I could write this again and again.**

52

I'm still doing most of the
talking, your heart
so loud in mine.

53

**Look through the letters
of your name.
You see me too. Just us.**

54

**Your absent body
more here.
Memory more present.**

55

Please, one touch.
Two.
Many.

56

**The brush to soothe
now
renders our rent.**

57

**A new kitten
in the house
awakens you everywhere.**

58

Ascension is no place
for a cat.
Come down here.

59

**Not one nook or cranny
escaped your nosiness
your holiness.**

60

You are famous now
under apple boughs
for sad people everywhere.

61

Never did want to fix
your blocked tear duct.
Can't shut mine now.

62

**Warming low October sun
on my ear.
All that time you did this.**

63

Up the stairs, 'round the door,
on the pillow, you
always around.

64

Come around my chair here.
Jump up.
Let me brush you to death.

65

**Having heard about you
before, your presence brought
everything. Absence, even more.**

66

**Dwelling mate, I can hear
that percolating puffing
when you are interested.**

67

I cannot think you up.
I have put you down.
Only feelings matter now.

68

Isolated, far from home,
we are now
one and many.

69

Did somebody say my cat died?
We all know what
that means but cannot say.

70

**Something happened between us
before I said or thought
anything. You too?**

71

**Just about every morning
We three ending up in
one bed—you, chest, her, back.**

Duncan lived and traveled with Sonnets for a dozen years while he was teaching, preaching and writing. He is known for "Quiet Fire," his writing and radio broadcasts on Abraham Lincoln.

He lives now with his late wife's mysterious cat named Bounce in Belfast, Maine.

www.ingramcontent.com/pod-product-compliance
Lightning Source LLC
Chambersburg PA
CBHW030824060726

47590CB00004B/1384